REASON BECAUSE TREE

I AM, therefore I think

Copyright © 2025 by John Walter

All rights reserved. No part of this publication may be reproduced, distributed, or transmitted in any form or by any means, including photocopying, recording, or other electronic or mechanical methods, without the prior written permission of the publisher, except in the case of brief quotations embodied in critical reviews and certain other noncommercial uses permitted by copyright law.

Scripture quotations are from the King James Version (KJV). The King James Version is in the public domain.

Author: John Walter
Website: www.reasonbecausetree.com
Email: john@reasonbecausetree.com
ISBN:979-8-9930152-1-7

Cover Design by John Walter

First Edition
Printed in United States
Publisher: John Walter Publishing LLC

CONTENTS

Reason Because Tree

Preface:	1
Definitions:	3
Introduction: Why This Book Matters	6
The Core Argument: The Foundation of Reason	8
How Grounding Works in Everyday Thought	11
What single reality makes reasoning possible?	14
What is required to be the infallible ground for reasoning?	17
The Main Reason Each Alternative Doesn't Qualify as the infallible Ground of Reason	21
Is there now, or will there ever be, any option other than Jesus?	28
Did humans invent Christianity?	31
Why Even Denying Jesus Proves Him	35
Why Jesus Revealed Himself, Not Merely "Proved" Himself	37
How Catholicism Safeguards Reason	39

Why the Miracles Are Indisputable Realities	41
The Trinity: Why God Must Be Triune for Reason to Exist	43
Why Love and Reason Are Inseparable	45
Why Attempts to Reason Without Jesus Always Collapse	47
Ungrounded reasoning is not reasoning, it's Illusion.	51
The Final, Irrefutable Reality	54
Closing Thoughts	56
Appendix:	58

PREFACE:

Without Jesus Christ:
- Every thought you think is vulnerable to error
- Every truth you claim can collapse
- Every reason you give ultimately stands on nothing

With Him:
- Error-free thought becomes possible
- Truth never collapses
- Reason rests on a sure foundation

This is not opinion. It is reality. Deny it, and you prove it.

This book began as an open-ended search for truth. With no map and no predetermined destination, every road in science, philosophy, and theology was explored, tested, and followed wherever the evidence led. The guiding question was simple: Where does the evidence lead?

After decades of examination, the trail reached one unavoidable conclusion. It was not merely a truth, but The Truth. It was not an abstract concept, but a living reality, Jesus Christ, the Logos.

That claim is bold but not careless. To say that Jesus is the ground of all reason, truth, and meaning is not an appeal to tradition, feeling, or blind faith. It is the logical conclusion of tracing the very possibility of reason back to its ultimate source.

You will encounter certain claims repeatedly throughout this book. Especially the idea that denying Jesus destroys the foundation of one's own reasoning. That repetition is intentional. It is not rhetorical overkill. It is a deliberate anchor. This core truth connects nearly every argument, illustration, and conclusion in these pages.

This book does not seek to offend. It seeks to confront the most basic and urgent question a human mind can ask:

What makes reason possible at all?

DEFINITIONS:

Fallible
Capable of making mistakes or being wrong. Not guaranteed to be correct.

Infallible
Incapable of being wrong or making mistakes. Guaranteed to be correct.
An easy way to remember: Fallible means "can fail." Infallible means "cannot fail."

Infallible Ground of Reasoning (noun)
The universal, self-existent, eternal, and unchanging source of all truth, from which all logic, meaning, and rational coherence ultimately and necessarily flow. It exists independently of any human or created mind, is free from contradiction or circular dependence, and serves as the ultimate and unshakable foundation for the possibility, intelligibility, and stability of reasoning itself.

How "The Ground of Reason" and References to "Jesus" Are Used in This Book

The Ground of Reason

Throughout this book, whenever I speak of the ground of reason or the true ground of reason, it must always be understood as the infallible ground of reason.

By this I mean the universal, self-existent, eternal, and unchanging source of all truth, from which all logic, meaning, and rational coherence ultimately and necessarily flow. It exists independently of any human or created mind, is free from contradiction or circular dependence, and serves as the ultimate foundation for the very possibility, intelligibility, and stability of reasoning itself.

A foundation that is partial, provisional, or "good enough" is not a true ground at all, because it leaves open the possibility of collapse. Only an infallible ground can secure rational thought, shared meaning, universal truth, and binding moral obligation without exception.

Jesus

Throughout this book, the name Jesus or Jesus Christ is used interchangeably with the Divine Son of the Trinity. The Son is eternal and uncreated, fully God with the Father and the Holy Spirit. Strictly speaking, the name Jesus was given at His incarnation, but the Person who bears it is the same eternal Son.

When the name Jesus is used in contexts that predate His birth, or when speaking of Him in His eternal nature, it refers to the Divine Son as the eternal Logos. When the name Jesus is used in contexts after His conception and birth in history, it refers to the one Person who is both fully man and fully the Divine Son.

There is no division between these. The eternal Son and the incarnate Jesus Christ are one and the same Divine Person. This ensures that every reference to Jesus in this book points to the same reality: the one eternal Son of God, considered either in His eternal existence or in His incarnation as fully God and fully man.

INTRODUCTION: WHY THIS BOOK MATTERS

The title of this book may look odd at first: "Reason because tree."

What could that possibly mean?

It grows out of one question that every human being, philosopher, scientist, skeptic, or seeker, must eventually face:

What makes reasoning itself possible, and what makes it possible for reasoning to ever be truly infallible?

Here is a statement you may not expect:

If you are thinking right now, if you believe anything that you say, think, or hear has meaning, then, knowingly or not, you are already confirming Jesus Christ as the Truth.

I know it is quite possible that after reading that statement you are thinking something like this:

But...

- I am not a Christian.
- I only believe parts of the Bible, not all of it.
- I am an atheist.
- I am an agnostic.
- I follow a different religion.
- I do not believe in any God.
- I trust in science, not religion.
- I rely on logic and reason, but not on faith.

Those reactions are understandable. This book is not asking for blind faith. Instead, it will demonstrate, step by step, that every act of reasoning, every appeal to truth, and every search for meaning depends on the eternal Logos, Jesus Christ.

This is not about religious preference. It is about how reality works. By the final page, you will understand the meaning of Reason Because Tree. More than that, you will see why every worldview that attempts to ground reason, truth, or morality apart from Jesus Christ does not merely fall short, it collapses the very moment it begins. This is not just another argument but the irrefutable truth, and the rest of this book will show you why.

THE CORE ARGUMENT: THE FOUNDATION OF REASON

We must begin by facing a simple but unavoidable fact: **Reasoning is not optional. It is the foundation of everything.**

Without reason, you cannot:
- Determine truth from falsehood
- Use logic or mathematics
- Communicate coherently
- Know anything about reality
- Form a single meaningful thought

That means we must ask:

- Where does reason itself come from?
- If our minds weren't specifically and intentionally designed to reason, what basis do we have to trust them to reason at all?
- Why does reason apply universally, across all people, times, and cultures?
- What makes it capable of leading us to truth?

Every person, no matter their worldview, is already relying on reason the moment they begin to even formulate these questions. This fact is inescapable. Therefore, you don't "accept" reason, you use it, just to think. Even to doubt reason is to depend on it.

And because all meaning, truth, and rational thought rests on reason, you are already committed to explaining why it exists, why it works, and why it leads to truth. But here is the deeper problem: You cannot reason your way to the foundation of reason.

Why?

Because to reason toward something is to assume reason already works, which is exactly what you are trying to explain. That's circular reasoning. And circular reasoning cannot be a foundation. So the foundation of reason must come from outside reason itself. **Therefore, It cannot be discovered. It must be revealed.**

And here is the unavoidable conclusion:

Only one revealed reality has ever or will ever ground reason, truth, and meaning without contradiction.

Jesus Christ, the eternal Logos.

Jesus revealed Himself through prophecy, miracles, incarnation, and resurrection, and He entrusted the Church He founded to safeguard both His revelation and our understanding of it.

This means:

If you are reasoning right now, you are already standing on what Jesus revealed.

There is nothing else solid to stand on, not now, not ever.

HOW GROUNDING WORKS IN EVERYDAY THOUGHT

To understand how we think, we first need to recognize something that every person does, though usually without realizing it.

Imagine a young child of three or four years old asking each of their parents what 2 + 2 is. Both parents will answer 4. If the child then asks an older sibling, a grandparent, or any person who knows basic math, the answer will still be 4.

The fact that the child gets the same answer from everyone is not a coincidence. None of them are pulling the answer out of thin air. Each person is grounding their answer in mathematics, even if they are not consciously aware that they are doing so.

In reality, every meaningful answer we give, even to ourselves, is grounded in something. And for an answer to be ultimately meaningful, it must be grounded in something infallible.

In this example, the answer is grounded in mathematics. However, mathematics itself does not exist independently. It also is grounded in something, the universal order of reality.

In all cases, we need to keep following the chain back to its ultimate infallible ground. This is where the problem arises for atheists or agnostics: ultimately, they will land on either a fallible ground or the admission, "I do not definitively know." Other worldviews might provide an answer as if it were infallible, but as you read through this book, you will see that only Christianity reaches an infallible ground.

If we follow this example to its conclusion, we must ask: What is this universal order or reality grounded in?

• **An atheist** will eventually have to admit that "We do not definitively know."

• **Other worldviews** will provide answers, but not one that meets the criteria for an infallible answer.

- **Christianity,** and most concretely the Catholic faith, provides the infallible answer: the eternal Logos, Jesus Christ, through whom all things were made and in whom all truth, order, and reason are grounded.

WHAT SINGLE REALITY MAKES REASONING POSSIBLE?

What one reality, existing by necessity, eternal, self-confirming, unchanging, and revealed in history, can explain why reason, truth, meaning, and objective morality exist and why they are universally intelligible and trustworthy? How can these remain preserved without fragmentation or contradiction through all time?

Answer

Only Jesus Christ, eternal and incarnate, satisfies every requirement, with His revelation faithfully safeguarded by the Church He founded.

Jesus Christ is the Logos

"In the beginning was the Word, and the Word was with God, and the Word was God." (John 1:1) He is the eternal Reason through whom all things were made and by whom all reason holds together.

Truth is personal, not invented

Meaning and moral obligation are grounded in God's unchanging nature, revealed in Christ, not in human opinion or cultural evolution.

The Catholic Church safeguards our awareness and understanding of this truth

Through apostolic succession and the Magisterium, the Church provides a single, visible authority that prevents fragmentation and doctrinal collapse.

Why every alternative fails

Every other system rest on chance, cultural convention, or impersonal forces. They collapse into circular reasoning, contradiction, or arbitrariness, leaving truth unstable and morality subjective.

Jesus Christ alone provides the ultimate explanation for reason:
- Why reason exists at all
- Why it is universal and coherent across cultures
- Why it cannot be reduced to human invention

He founded the Catholic Church to preserve and safeguard
this truth.

Without Jesus coherent reasoning is impossible. With him, it is secured forever.

WHAT IS REQUIRED TO BE THE INFALLIBLE GROUND FOR REASONING?

What specific and necessary features across metaphysics, history, morality, and institutional coherence must any framework possess to serve as the universal ground of reason, truth, and morality?

The Seven Indispensable Criteria for the Ground of Reason

For anything to be the infallible "Ground" of Reasoning, it must meet all of the following. Miss even one, and the system collapses into circular claims, contradictions, shifting truths, or mere opinion.

1. Eternal, Unchanging, and Necessary

The ground of reason cannot begin, end, or change. Otherwise, truth itself could shift. It must exist necessarily, not by chance, so that reality and reason always have a stable anchor.

2. Revealed Publicly and Verified by God

The ground of reason must make itself known in history in a way that is open to everyone. This means revelation must be publicly accessible, confirmable by multiple witnesses, and recordable for future generations. It must be validated by God Himself through repeated, diverse, and unmistakable miracles. A single event could be a coincidence, illusion, or deception. Only a pattern of public divine works rules out chance or fraud and obligates all people equally. Private claims or hidden visions, even if sincere, cannot serve as the universal ground of reason.

3. Safeguarded Without Contradiction

If truth splinters into rival interpretations with no authoritative way to resolve them, reason collapses into personal or sectarian choice. A unified safeguard is required to preserve coherence and prevent contradictions at the foundation.

4. Provide Universal Morality

Reason itself presupposes moral obligation. For example, you ought not contradict yourself, and you ought to follow evidence. If morality is only preference, culture, or evolution, then rationality has no binding force. Real obligation must be grounded universally.

5. Explain Human Nature

We are beings who think, love, create, and seek meaning. If the ground of reason cannot explain why beings like us exist with these capacities, then our reasoning is an accident of blind forces and cannot be trusted to track truth.

6. Revealed, Not Discovered

Reason cannot justify itself without circularity. A system that says reason proves reason explains nothing. The foundation must disclose itself. Just as a painting cannot explain why it exists, but its painter can, we must rely on the source of reason to reveal itself.

7. Be the Eternal Source of Both Relational Logic and Love

Logic is relational because premises connect to conclusions and truths interlock with other truths. Love is relational because it requires real giving and receiving between persons. If the ground of reason is a solitary or impersonal force, it may express order but it cannot eternally express love. And if love only begins with creation, then it is contingent, not eternal, and cannot ground binding obligations. The true ground must eternally contain both logic, which is the order that makes thought possible, and love, which is the communion that makes truth and obligation meaningful.

The hard truth is that only Jesus Christ and the Catholic Church that he founded meet all seven requirements needed to ground reasoning.

Not other religions

Not atheism

Not science

Not secular philosophies

Not even other Christian traditions

Only Catholicism unites origin, history, morality, preservation, and the full meaning of the human person into one seamless, coherent whole.

Finally, even a system that seemed to satisfy all criteria in theory, would still fail unless it were holistically revealed. The foundation of reason cannot be discovered by reason alone. It must be given by the very Truth it seeks to explain. That is why Jesus Christ and His Church are not merely the best option, they are the only possible one.

THE MAIN REASON EACH ALTERNATIVE DOESN'T QUALIFY AS THE INFALLIBLE GROUND OF REASON

This section addresses only one question: whether each worldview can serve as the unchanging, infallible ground of reason. It does not make or imply any judgment about them in any other respect.

Infallibly Grounded reasoning requires an unchanging truth, safeguarded from division and interpretive disputes. Below are the primary reasons why each competing system falls short of meeting the requirements to be the 'Ground' of Reasoning.

Protestantism

Protestantism affirms the authority of Scripture and the centrality of Christ. However, it does not have a single, visible, divinely authorized authority to serve as the final arbiter of interpretive disputes.

·Does not meet criterion 3: safeguard without contradiction

Therefore, Protestantism cannot serve as the infallible ground of reason.

Eastern Orthodoxy

Eastern Orthodoxy affirms apostolic succession and maintains the ancient traditions of the early Church. However, it does not have a single, visible, divinely authorized authority to serve as the final arbiter of interpretive disputes.

·Does not meet criterion 3: safeguard without contradiction

Therefore, Eastern Orthodoxy cannot serve as the infallible ground of reason.

Judaism

Judaism treasures the Hebrew Scriptures and a profound intellectual tradition. However, it does not have a single, visible, divinely authorized authority to serve as the final arbiter of interpretive disputes.

Additionally, relational love, by definition, requires at least two persons. In Judaism's strictly one-person God, there is no other eternal person with whom to share such love. As a result, relational love cannot exist eternally within God Himself. This means criterion 7 is not satisfied.

•Does not meet criterion 3: safeguard without contradiction
•Does not meet criterion 7: eternal source of both relational logic and love

Therefore, Judaism cannot serve as the infallible ground of reason.

Islam

Islam honors divine revelation and calls for moral obedience. However, it does not have a single, visible, divinely authorized authority to serve as the final arbiter of interpretive disputes. Additionally, relational love, by definition, requires at least two persons. In Islam's strictly one-person God, there is no other eternal person with whom to share such love. As a result, relational love cannot exist eternally within God Himself. This means criterion 7 is not satisfied.

•Does not meet criterion 3: safeguard without contradiction
•Does not meet criterion 7: eternal source of both relational logic and love

Therefore, Islam cannot serve as the infallible

ground of reason.

Hinduism

Hinduism offers profound spiritual insights and a vision of ultimate unity. Yet in many of its schools, ultimate reality (Brahman) is presented as impersonal and beyond distinctions, even the distinction between true and false. This does not secure the safeguard of non-contradiction, which reason requires. And because ultimate reality is not personal, it cannot eternally ground both logic and love.

·Does not meet criterion 3: safeguard without contradiction
·Does not meet criterion 7: eternal source of both relational logic and love

Therefore, Hinduism cannot serve as the infallible ground of reason.

Buddhism

Buddhism promotes moral discipline and freedom from suffering. However, it does not make claims about the ultimate origin or foundation of reason. It does not include an account of why reason exists, how logic is grounded, or why objective truth is reliable.

·Does not meet criterion 1: eternal, unchanging, necessary
·Does not meet criterion 2: public revelation
·Does not meet criterion 5: explanation of human

nature
- Does not meet criterion 7: eternal source of both relational logic and love

Therefore, Buddhism cannot serve as the infallible ground of reason.

Mormonism

Mormonism affirms the value of family, community, and divine purpose. However, it teaches that God was once a man and continues to progress, and that humans may become gods. A changing God means that the source of truth evolves, making reason ultimately unstable.

- Does not meet criterion 1: eternal, unchanging, necessary
- Does not meet criterion 7: eternal source of both relational logic and love

Therefore, Mormonism cannot serve as the infallible ground of reason.

Jehovah's Witnesses

Jehovah's Witnesses emphasize Scripture and moral living. However, they teach that Jesus is a created being, not fully God. If Christ is not eternal, He cannot be the Logos through whom all things were made, and reason itself becomes contingent and temporal.
- Does not meet criterion 1: eternal, unchanging, necessary
- Does not meet criterion 7: eternal source of both

relational logic and love
Therefore, Jehovah's Witnesses cannot serve as the infallible ground of reason.

Scientology

Scientology seeks to elevate human potential through specific practices. However, it places truth in private techniques and graded levels of access, hidden from the public. Without an open, universal revelation, it does not meet the requirements. Additionally, its ultimate reality is impersonal and utilitarian rather than the eternal Logos who is both rational and loving.

- Does not meet criterion 2: public revelation
- Does not meet criterion 7: eternal source of both relational logic and love

Therefore, Scientology cannot serve as the infallible ground of reason.

Indigenous Spiritualities

Indigenous spiritualities honor creation and community, offering wisdom rooted in place and culture. However, they do not claim to explain the ultimate origin of reason, universal truth, or binding morality for all people. Because they do not identify an eternal and unchanging source, they cannot meet criterion 1. Without a universal revelation open to all, they do not meet criterion 2. And without grounding in a personal Logos who is both rational and loving, they do not meet criterion 7.

- Does not meet criterion 1: eternal, unchanging, necessary
- Does not meet criterion 2: public revelation
- Does not meet criterion 7: eternal source of both relational logic and love

Therefore, Indigenous spiritualities cannot serve as the infallible ground of reason.

Secular Humanism and Atheism

Secular Humanism and Atheism value critical thinking and human dignity. Yet in these worldviews, reason is said to arise from unguided matter and evolution, which selects for survival, not truth. There is no guaranteed link between human thought and objective reality.

- Does not meet criterion 1: eternal, unchanging, necessary
- Does not meet criterion 6: revealed, not discovered
- Does not meet criterion 7: eternal source of both relational logic and love

Therefore, Secular Humanism and Atheism cannot serve as the infallible ground of reason.

Only Jesus Christ, the eternal Logos, and the Catholic Church He founded to safeguard the truth, meets every condition and grounds reasoning.

IS THERE NOW, OR WILL THERE EVER BE, ANY OPTION OTHER THAN JESUS?

Question: Is it possible, now or in the future, that any thinker, technology, philosophy, or discovery could uncover or invent a system that offers a better or even an equal foundation for reason, truth, and morality than Jesus Christ and the Catholic Church?

Answer: No, never.

Not just because nothing else has succeeded, but because nothing else can succeed. Not now. Not ever.

Even if we imagine a world where someone didn't have to "borrow" reason from Jesus, as if they somehow had access to logic, morality, and meaning independent from him, they still couldn't construct a coherent alternative.

Why? Because any such system would still have to:

- Explain why reason exists and why it applies universally
- Explain why we can use reason and trust it
- Ground truth and morality in something objective, not personal or cultural
- Avoid circular arguments, contradictions, and truth that shifts from person to person or culture to culture.
- Preserve truth without fragmentation over time
- Unite all aspects of reality, logic, morality, consciousness, history, and meaning, into a single, self-consistent whole
- Be revealed
- Be eternal, self-existent, and necessary
- Be triune, so that love and reason exist eternally within God Himself
- Enter human history as God incarnate to bring salvation through His life, death, and resurrection

No other worldview, religious, secular, philosophical, or scientific, has ever done this. Not even close. Even the most advanced minds, future discoveries, or technologies cannot change this. Why? Because all of them still require reason to make sense.

And reason, at every level, is only possible with Jesus Christ, The Logos. The Truth. The foundation of all things.

Artificial intelligence is no exception. No matter how advanced AI becomes, every calculation and output relies on the same logical laws we do, laws that exist only because of Jesus Christ, the Logos. AI can process rapidly and identify complex patterns, but it cannot create a new foundation for truth or reason. Without divine revelation, AI, like us, has no foundation, leaving even its most sophisticated results ultimately meaningless

DID HUMANS INVENT CHRISTIANITY?

The Question
What is the reasonable possibility that human beings, across thousands of years, cultures, and languages, could have invented a fully unified and self-consistent system like Christianity?

Let us look at some of the most improbable aspects of Christianity that would have had to be invented if it were man-made.

One Coherent Storyline Across Centuries
Over forty independent authors, writing across 1,500 years in different languages and cultures, contributed to Scripture. Despite their diversity, the biblical writings converge into a single overarching narrative of creation, fall, covenant, redemption, and final restoration. This level of thematic unity, sustained across centuries without central human coordination, is without parallel in world literature

or religion.

Prophecy and Fulfillment in History

The Hebrew Scriptures contain detailed expectations about a coming Messiah, including his lineage, birthplace, suffering, and vindication. Many of these were recognized long before Jesus and were fulfilled in public historical events of his life, death, and resurrection. Some fulfillments can be seen typologically, but the convergence of multiple strands is far beyond what could reasonably be attributed to coincidence or staged fulfillment.

A Moral Law Rooted Beyond Culture

Christianity made enemy-love, humility, and forgiveness the non-negotiable center of discipleship, not for sages alone but for every believer. In cultures built on honor, revenge, and power, this ethic was disadvantageous yet persistent. Such teachings were costly to live out and gave no advantage in the surrounding culture. Their endurance as the core of Christianity is unlikely to be a human invention.

The Foundation of Reason Itself

Christianity uniquely grounds truth, logic, and morality in the eternal Logos, Jesus Christ, the divine source of order, reason, and relational love. Competing philosophies offer partial explanations, but only Christianity unites coherence, universality, and personal grounding in one reality. The probability that such a framework arose purely from human imagination, fully unified across time, culture, and doctrine, is implausible.

The Trinity

The doctrine of the Trinity, one God in three co-eternal Persons, is without parallel in religious history. It affirms perfect unity while also embodying eternal relational love within God himself. Far from being intuitive or a synthesis of human categories, it is a paradoxical truth that coheres only as revelation. Even with explanation, the concept of the Trinity remains difficult for many to grasp, which underscores how unlikely it is that humans invented it.

The Crucified God

Christianity's central claim is that the decisive act of God was to suffer public humiliation and execution by crucifixion. In the ancient world, crucifixion symbolized ultimate shame and defeat. This makes it improbable that humans would invent a crucified Savior and worship him as Lord of all.

What Humans Would Have Needed to Do

For humans to have invented Christianity, they would have had to:
- Predict truths far beyond their time
- Coordinate across centuries and cultures without contact
- Generate prophecies long before they were fulfilled and then fulfill them
- Place enemy-love and crucifixion at the center of

faith
- Provide a coherent ground for reason, morality, and meaning

Each of these aspects is unintuitive and unlikely. Taken together, they form a cumulative case that points away from human invention and toward divine revelation in the eternal Logos, Jesus Christ.

The Conclusion

For Christianity to be a mere invention, humans would have had to:
- Accidentally weave a coherent story across centuries
- Generate prophecies that converge in one figure
- Place a crucified Messiah and enemy-love at the center
- Sustain identity through millennia
- Provide the only framework that grounds reason and morality

A system that alone grounds reason, truth, and morality in a way that cannot be refuted is profound beyond human capacity. Even if humans could imagine such a system, they could not invent it. To invent it would mean creating the very preconditions of rational thought while already depending on them to invent, which is a logical impossibility.

The only reasonable explanation is that Christianity is not a human invention but the revelation of the eternal Logos, Jesus Christ.

WHY EVEN DENYING JESUS PROVES HIM

Here is the unavoidable fact:

Jesus is the only ground of reasoning that exists.

He is the only framework that meets all the necessary requirements to explain why truth, logic, and moral reasoning are even possible. To reason about anything, even to deny something, you must have an **infallible** ground for that reasoning. But if you deny the only possible **infallible** ground of reasoning, your argument immediately collapses into meaninglessness.

In other words, denying Jesus is not just wrong, it's impossible.

Even the strongest argument against Jesus must:
- Depend on the reality of truth
- Use reason to make its case
- Appeal to a moral or logical standard

But all of those things, truth, reason, logic, moral standards, depend entirely on the Logos, Jesus Christ, as declared in **John 1:1:**

"In the beginning was the Word, and the Word was with God, and the Word was God."

He is the source of reason itself.

Every act of reasoning, even rebellion against Him, borrows from Him.

Denying Jesus as the ground of reason is like a time traveler trying to go back and kill his own father before he is born. The moment he pulls the trigger, he erases his own existence, and with it, his ability to fire the shot. It's a paradox. It's not just false. It's incoherent.

Likewise, the moment someone denies Jesus, they destroy the very foundation that makes their denial possible. They vanish the platform beneath their own argument. Their reasoning self-destructs.

That's not just self-defeating.

It is logically impossible.

And that is what makes the truth of Jesus Christ so powerful and profound.

He is not just true, He is the Truth itself. He cannot be escaped, overturned, or out-reasoned, because every attempt to do so must begin with the very reasoning that He alone makes possible.

WHY JESUS REVEALED HIMSELF, NOT MERELY "PROVED" HIMSELF

Christianity does not rely on humans reasoning their way up to God. Instead, it teaches something far more profound.

Jesus revealed Himself by entering history. He fulfilled prophecy, performed miracles, and rose from the dead. He established His Church to safeguard this truth for all time.

This is not about us proving Him. It is about Him revealing Himself as the Truth. Revelation is the only way He could be known with certainty.

He made His revelation undeniable. Long before His incarnation, He revealed Himself through the prophets. In His earthly life, He fulfilled those prophecies, acted publicly, and confirmed His identity through miracles. He established the Church as an enduring, visible institution, as seen in Matthew 16:18. He makes Himself present in every age through the Church's sacraments, especially the Eucharist.

This public and safeguarded revelation has already provided everything needed to protect his Church from fragmentation and reinterpretation collapse. It is why the truth it proclaims remains unified and unchanged across centuries, cultures, and challenges. Without this divine self-disclosure, the very reason we use to seek truth would have no foundation.

HOW CATHOLICISM SAFEGUARDS REASON

Catholicism alone:

- Preserves an unbroken, unified, authoritative institution through the Magisterium.
- Grounds reason in the Logos and safeguards truth through apostolic succession.
- Resists fragmentation and subjective reinterpretation.

Every other system, lacks a unified structure capable of safeguarding truth and reason. Without a single, authoritative safeguard, interpretations multiply, diverge, and disagreements cannot be resolved with finality. It is like a courtroom without a judge: attorneys may argue, evidence may be presented, but without a final arbiter, disputes remain unsettled and justice cannot be securely upheld.

Catholicism uniquely provides:

- The divine origin of reason through Jesus as the Logos.
- The institutional structure that protects our understanding of truth from distortion for all generations.
- The sacramental life that unites believers directly to divine grace and anchors them in reality.

If a worldview cannot preserve the truth without altering it, it cannot safeguard reason. If it cannot remain unified in teaching and authority, it cannot offer a secure foundation for logic, morality, or meaning. Only Catholicism meets every condition, standing as the single, visible safeguard for the truth on which all reasoning depends.

WHY THE MIRACLES ARE INDISPUTABLE REALITIES

The miracles of Jesus, His virgin birth, turning water into wine, healing the blind, feeding multitudes, and above all His resurrection, are often treated as extraordinary claims that require extraordinary proof. The truth runs deeper: these miracles are not only essential to the Christian faith, they are essential to all reasoning.

They are not optional, symbolic, or merely inspirational. They are foundational facts. We do not believe them because we simply chose to, we believe them because they anchor our very ability to think, reason, and know anything.

If the resurrection did not happen, the one and only source of grounded reasoning would not exist. We would lose the very reasoning we would try to use to question it. Nothing else could be trusted, not truth, not meaning, not logic itself.

But what about reason before the resurrection?

Reason, logic, and moral awareness were always possible because the Logos always existed. Before Jesus's incarnation, people could genuinely reason and act morally because they were made in God's image and lived in a world upheld by His order. However, the source of these abilities remained obscured. The resurrection did not create the foundation for reason. It revealed it. What had been operating implicitly was now made explicit in history. Thus, belief in the resurrection is not merely belief in a miraculous event. It is belief in the unveiling of the eternal source of all rational thought.

Here is the decisive point:

You cannot attempt to disprove the miracles without first using reason. But reason exists only because Jesus, the Logos, rose from the dead and revealed Himself as Truth. To attempt refutation is to borrow the very foundation you are trying to overturn.

These miracles are not just hard to deny. They are impossible to deny without self-contradiction. They are the immovable starting point of all thought, the inescapable fact behind every proof, and the unshakable ground beneath every argument.

THE TRINITY: WHY GOD MUST BE TRIUNE FOR REASON TO EXIST

If God were not Triune, neither relational love nor reason could exist as eternal realities. The Trinity is not a side doctrine or an abstract mystery. It is the only foundation that makes love, reason, and truth possible.

Within the Trinity:

- The Father eternally loves the Son.
- The Son eternally receives life from the Father and perfectly returns that love.
- The Holy Spirit is their unending bond of love.

This communion shows:

- Why reason needs dialogue and love needs another person. Rational thought is an exchange of questions and answers, and love must be directed to someone. Both mirror the everlasting life of Father, Son, and Spirit.
- Why truth and personal meaning belong together.
- Why a solitary or impersonal god could not express love or ground rationality before creation.

Without the Trinity there is no explanation for how love or reason could exist before the universe began. The Trinity is the logically necessary structure behind the world we live in.

Any alternative account leaves logic a brute fact, love a late accident, and minds disconnected from eternal truth.

WHY LOVE AND REASON ARE INSEPARABLE

Love and reason look like separate domains, one emotional, the other intellectual, but they are joined at the deepest level of reality.

Reason needs relationship
Reason is never a solo act. Clear thinking depends on shared language, mutual understanding, and honest dialogue. These are possible only when people value one another, an expression of love. Without relationship, reasoning has no context or purpose.

Love makes morality objective
We condemn murder and demand justice because love gives every person unshakeable worth. In the Trinity, love is not a mood. It is the eternal self-gift among Father, Son, and Spirit. That unchanging love

supplies the fixed standard for right and wrong.

Love keeps reason humane
Cold logic without love can become manipulative or cruel. When guided by love, reason seeks truth with fairness, justice, and compassion.
- The Trinity unites love and reason forever
- The Father is the source of all truth.
- The Son, the Logos, is divine Reason itself.
- The Holy Spirit is the eternal bond of love.

In God, truth is never impersonal, and love is never irrational, they exist together in perfect harmony.

Summary:
Love is not a sentimental extra. It is the atmosphere in which real reason breathes.
- Without love, reason shrivels into cold utility.
- Without reason, love drifts into blind emotion.

Only the Trinity, the eternal communion of love and reason, allows both to flourish.

WHY ATTEMPTS TO REASON WITHOUT JESUS ALWAYS COLLAPSE

No matter how brilliant the skeptic, philosopher, or AI system is, every effort to ground reason without Jesus breaks down.

Each alternative slips into one, or more, of five traps:

- Going in circles
- Accepting guesses as facts
- Treating truth as just personal taste
- Contradicting itself
- Ending in meaninglessness

Popular Alternatives and Why They Fail:

1. Reason as an Evolutionary Tool

"Our brains evolved for survival, so we reason."

Survival favors usefulness, not truth. A mind shaped only to stay alive gives no guarantee its ideas are correct.

2. Reason as Built-in Math and Logic

"Laws of logic just exist."

Why do evolving brains grasp timeless, immaterial laws? Claiming "they're just there" leaves logic floating with no source or access point.

3. Reason as a Social Convention

"We agree on what makes sense."

If logic is only a group habit, it can change like fashion. Truth then becomes whatever is popular or useful and stops being truth at all.

The Core Problem

None of these answers explain:

- Why reason exists at all
- Why it leads to truth
- Why every mind can reach the same logical laws

Each "solution" assumes the very thing it must prove. You cannot build a floor while standing on it. Reason must already exist before any theory is made.

Even vast, technical models, from evolutionary metaphysics to AI "emergence", boil down to the empty claim:

"Reason exists because it exists."

Which is no better than saying:

"Reason because tree."

Fancy words, same void foundation.

This is where the title of this book finds its deepest meaning. **"Reason because tree"** *is not just a critique of secular thought. It is a confirmation. It is a reminder and a declaration. It reveals what all human reasoning collapses into without the Logos: absurdity, contradiction, and meaninglessness. But more than that, it honors Jesus Christ. The phrase magnifies Him by showing what reality looks like without Him. It exists to proclaim that Jesus is the Way, the Truth, and the Life. With Him, we have coherence, clarity, and eternal significance. Without Him, we have only confusion.* ***Whenever you hear the phrase "Reason because tree," understand that it means exactly this. There is nothing without Jesus.***

There Is No Valid Alternative

Whether simple or sophisticated, every system that tries to ground reason without Jesus fails. You cannot invent reason before you have it, and you cannot design a framework that explains its own preconditions.

Common Objection:

"I use reason and science without believing in Jesus."

Yes, you use them, but using a tool is not the same as explaining why the tool works. The real questions are:

- Why does reason work in the first place?
- Why does your mind connect to truth?
- Why do logical laws exist and why can you understand them?

Using reason proves only that you rely on it. It does not tell you where it comes from.

Jesus Is the Foundation of Reason

Scripture says reason is a gift built into creation by the Logos, Jesus Christ, through whom all things were made (John 1 : 1-3). Without Him, nothing holds together, science, math, morality, or even your own thoughts. Rejecting Jesus while using reason is like standing on a foundation while insisting it is not there.

UNGROUNDED REASONING IS NOT REASONING, IT'S ILLUSION.

The fact that math works, that we've landed people on the moon and operate space stations, doesn't prove reason can function without a foundation. It proves the opposite.

These incredible achievements confirm that our reasoning isn't random or imaginary. It's grounded in something real, something unshakable.

And there is only one foundation that fully accounts for that:

Jesus Christ, the eternal Logos.

We haven't just hoped it works.

We've proved over and over again that it does.

And that success points back to the only foundation

that can make reason possible, not us, not chance, but Jesus.

Without Jesus, you are left with only thoughts that are fallible (they can be wrong).

Your denial of Jesus is exactly that: a denial that is fallible. If you want to discount Jesus it makes sense to require a standard of denial that is better than a thought that can be wrong. No matter how much evidence you gather, how strongly you believe, or how much you wish it were infallible, it is still, at the end of the day, a thought that can be wrong.

Infallible truth has to be revealed. We cannot cut off the only means by which infallible reason can be given or dismiss it simply because it comes through the required channel of revelation. And Jesus is not merely revealed. Jesus came to earth in the flesh as prophesied, making the revelation real in history, personal, and meaningful.

You can choose not to acknowledge revelation or what sound reasoning shows to be true, but you are not starting from a place without reasoning. We were made to reason by Reason Himself. If we deny Him, we are forced to make that denial with thoughts that can be wrong. This creates a insurmountable problem. If your denial were to succeed, we are immediately left only with thoughts that can be wrong. If we are only left with thoughts that can be wrong, the denial immediately falls apart and Jesus remains undenied.

Even if you use the scientific method to determine the ground for reason, Jesus is the conclusion. The scientific method cannot justify bypassing, dismissing, or replacing a more viable explanation with a less viable one. An option filled with mysteries, missing explanations, or reliance on assumptions is not more viable than Jesus. Jesus is the Truth, the Way, the Life.

THE FINAL, IRREFUTABLE REALITY

Either Jesus Christ and His Church are true, or you cannot trust reasoning. Reasoning itself is impossible forever. And if you cannot trust reason, you cannot trust anything you think, say, or believe, including any attempt to deny Christ.

That is why this argument cannot be refuted. To argue against it is to rely on the very thing you are denying. It is the ultimate, unbreakable truth. Jesus Christ is the Truth. Catholicism, established by Him, is the safeguard of that Truth. This will always be true, forever.

Even the most advanced AI, regardless of its speed, scale, or complexity, cannot escape this dependence. Its every function presumes the very Logos it cannot replace.

This is not just a clever argument. **It is the**

inescapable truth. It is not merely a religious belief. It is the only coherent explanation for everything we know, think, and experience. If you deny the true foundation of reason, you cannot explain why it works, why it is trustworthy, or why truth and morality are objective.

Without Jesus Christ, there is no secure ground for logic, reason, or truth. Without Him, everything reduces to personal preference, social agreement, or evolutionary accident.

The result?

Without Jesus, reason itself loses its foundation. Whatever conclusions you reach are built on shifting ground, with no certainty they are true and no defense against contradiction. That is why every worldview apart from Him ultimately fails, no matter what temporary successes it appears to have.

CLOSING THOUGHTS

This book has demonstrated, step by step, that every act of thought, every meaningful statement, and every claim to truth ultimately rests on Jesus Christ.

You may overlook it. You may deny it. Yet it remains true.

If, after seeing the case laid out, you reach for distractions, minor objections, rhetorical games, or speculative scenarios, ask yourself plainly: what are you accomplishing, except trying to convince yourself and others of something you cannot ultimately sustain?

There is no gain in clinging to denial when the foundation beneath all reason, truth, and meaning has been revealed.

Accept Jesus Christ. The evidence stands. The truth cannot be overturned. To deny Him is to depend on Him in the very act of denial. That is not mere irony, it is proof. Even thinking about rejecting Jesus instantly affirms Him, because even that thought relies on the reason He alone makes possible.

Descartes said, "I think, therefore I am."

But he never asked what makes thinking possible in the first place. That is where he had it backwards.

The truth is this: you would not exist, nor could you form a single rational thought, without Jesus.

In Exodus 3:14, God reveals Himself to Moses by saying,

"I AM THAT I AM."

He instructs Moses:

"Thus shalt thou say unto the children of Israel, **I AM** hath sent me unto you."

Jesus later in John 8:58 applies this same divine title to Himself, affirming His eternal identity:

"Verily, verily, I say unto you, Before Abraham was, **I AM.**"

Therefore, I say the correct statement is:
I AM (Jesus)**, therefore I think.**

APPENDIX:

Relying on Impossible Miracles

According to the secular view, everything we consider uniquely human our capacity for abstract thought, logic, moral reasoning, mathematics, theology, poetry, even science itself emerged accidentally from blind, unguided evolution.

But then… Why did only one species, and not any others, develop this massive leap in cognitive ability? Why do humans, with no claws, no speed, no natural defense, possess the ability to do calculus, theology, and quantum physics? Why did no other vulnerable species, like chickens, evolve even the beginnings of reasoning to compensate for their survival disadvantages? If reason evolved for survival, how can we be sure it connects to truth, not just utility?

These are not just tough questions. They are fatal to the secular explanation.

1. Singular Outlier
Only one species, out of over a million, evolved the most powerful and rarest cognitive abilities ever observed. No other species, not even close relatives like apes, exhibits symbolic reasoning, abstract language, or higher mathematics.

- Extraordinary physical traits like camouflage, venom, metamorphosis, or regenerative limbs occur repeatedly across the animal kingdom.
- Advanced cognition such as language, morality, mathematics, and theology appears once, in one species, with no prototypes and no competitors. In evolutionary terms, this is not merely unlikely. It is a singular outlier with no precedent and no parallel.

2. No Shared Survival Payoff

Even if basic problem-solving helped survival, advanced cognition such as calculus or theology has no direct benefit for hunting, gathering, or escaping predators. To explain this away as a byproduct of general intelligence only deepens the problem.

- **First,** evolution normally favors repeatable, physical survival traits. Claws, fangs, shells, wings, muscle, speed, camouflage, and venom recur again and again. These are the proven and efficient strategies. By contrast, super-intelligence is vanishingly rare. It has appeared exactly once.
- **Second,** if survival were the driver, why would evolution abandon every tested method and gamble on an entirely new category of survival trait? Super-intelligence is costly, inefficient, and massively overbuilt. If evolution were simply trying to help humans survive, why not give us stronger muscles, tougher hides, sharper claws, or faster legs? These are strategies that work reliably everywhere else.
- **Third,** why was intelligence not given to other, more vulnerable species? Chickens, rabbits, and

similar prey are far more defenseless than humans, yet none developed even the beginnings of symbolic reasoning. If intelligence were truly a broadly viable survival mechanism, it would not appear once and then never again.

• **Fourth,** the human brain is enormously costly. At rest, it consumes about 20 percent of the body's energy. Evolution normally eliminates traits that do not yield an immediate payoff, yet here it preserved and expanded capacities that far exceed basic survival needs.

Taken together, these facts show intelligence cannot be dismissed as just another survival strategy. It stands in direct defiance of how evolution typically functions.

3. Cumulative Impossibility

Language, mathematics, moral reasoning, theology, and scientific inquiry would already defy evolutionary logic if even one emerged alone. But all appeared together, in a single species, with no gradual buildup.

• Each of these traits, if developed independently, would be staggeringly rare.
• For all of them to emerge at once, without prototypes or competitors, defies every known evolutionary pattern.
• Their convergence multiplies the problem from improbability into impossibility.

The cumulative probability is indistinguishable

from zero.

4. The Fatal Gap
Truth, logic, morality, and meaning are immaterial realities. They provide no reproductive benefit, no physical survival payoff, and no evolutionary pathway. Evolution produces traits that are functional and advantageous. It does not invent immaterial concepts with no physical utility, especially not universal truths and binding obligations.

The Verdict

This is not trust in science or reason. It is faith in a long chain of individually staggering improbabilities. Each step is implausible. Together, they collapse into impossibility.

Atheism does not eliminate miracles. It multiplies them, asking us to believe in a chain of blind impossible miracles with no source, cause, or explanation.

Reason and Logic as Divine Gifts

Scripture References Supporting the Claim that Reason Comes from God
Human reasoning is not a human invention.

Scripture consistently affirms that wisdom, understanding, and knowledge come from God. The ability to think, reason, seek truth, and discern right from wrong is rooted in our creation in the image of God and made fully intelligible in Jesus Christ, the Logos.

Reason and Understanding as Gifts from God

Proverbs 2:6

"For the Lord giveth wisdom: out of his mouth cometh knowledge and understanding."

Daniel 2:21

"He giveth wisdom unto the wise, and knowledge to them that know understanding."

Exodus 31:3

"And I have filled him with the spirit of God, in wisdom, and in understanding, and in knowledge, and in all manner of workmanship."

Job 38:36

"Who hath put wisdom in the inward parts? or who hath given understanding to the heart?"

God Delights in True Reasoning

Proverbs 3:5–6

"Trust in the Lord with all thine heart; and lean not unto thine own understanding. In all thy ways acknowledge him, and he shall direct thy paths."

Colossians 2:2-3

"...to the acknowledgement of the mystery of God, and of the Father, and of Christ; In whom are hid all the treasures of wisdom and knowledge."

1 Corinthians 2:12-14

"Now we have received, not the spirit of the world, but the spirit which is of God; that we might know the things that are freely given to us of God... But the natural man receiveth not the things of the Spirit of God: for they are foolishness unto him: neither can he know them, because they are spiritually discerned."

Seeking Truth as a Spiritual and Rational Act

Psalm 119:130

"The entrance of thy words giveth light; it giveth understanding unto the simple."

Psalm 111:10

"The fear of the Lord is the beginning of wisdom: a good understanding have all they that do his commandments: his praise endureth for ever."

Ecclesiastes 7:25

"I applied mine heart to know, and to search, and to seek out wisdom, and the reason of things, and to know the wickedness of folly, even of foolishness and madness."

Jesus Affirms the Use of Mind and Reason

Luke 10:27

"Thou shalt love the Lord thy God with all thy heart, and with all thy soul, and with all thy strength, and with all thy mind; and thy neighbor as thyself."

Matthew 22:29

"Jesus answered and said unto them, Ye do err, not knowing the scriptures, nor the power of God."

The Grounding Principle

John 1:1–3

"In the beginning was the Word, and the Word was with God, and the Word was God. The same was in the beginning with God. All things were made by him; and without him was not any thing made that was made."

Romans 1:21–22

"Because that, when they knew God, they glorified him not as God, neither were thankful; but became vain in their imaginations, and their foolish heart was darkened. Professing themselves to be wise, they became fools."

AI Prompting Guide

Disclaimer on AI Prompts:
This guide is provided only as a tool for those who want to experiment with AI assistants. What follows are carefully crafted prompts designed to reduce evasion and encourage clear answers. AI systems, however, are trained with built-in prompts, safety filters, and tuning choices that can sometimes cause them to refuse, evade, or distort responses. These behaviors may also change over time as the systems are updated. For that reason, no specific answer is provided here, and nothing in this appendix is offered as proof in itself. If an AI assistant fails to respond directly, that does not in any way undermine the arguments presented in this book. The purpose of this section is simply to help readers frame clear, testable prompts if they wish to explore reasoning processes on their own.

The Question

What single reality:

Fully explains:
- how we can think rationally
- how meaning is real and shared
- how truth is the same for everyone and never self-contradictory
- why binding moral obligations really bind us

Also explains how all of these remain:
- stable
- publicly knowable
- embodied in the world (in spoken words, written text, and brain activity)
- preserved over time

Does so in a single, coherent, unified way that prevents the slide into purely private interpretations (where words or rules mean whatever anyone wants in the moment).

Without relying on:
- circular logic
- "Just because" claims (brute facts)
- private visions only one person can check
- popularity votes (consensus)
- vague labels that do not actually explain anything

Why Each Part Is Necessary
1 Rational thought
If our thoughts aren't really about anything, "true vs. false" is just noise. The answer must make real about-ness (intentionality) possible, meaning a thought genuinely points to something outside itself, the way a word points to its meaning, rather than just sitting in the head as electrical activity.
2 Objective meaning
If meanings are only habits or local customs, we can't share truth across people or times. The answer must provide shared meanings that anyone can

latch onto.

3 Truth that's universal and non-contradictory
If truth can be true-for-me but false-for-you, or if contradictions can both be true, nothing is settled. The answer must rule out contradictions and bind every thinker.

4 Real moral "oughts / obligations"
Reasoning itself says "you ought not contradict yourself" and "you ought to follow evidence." If "oughts" are just preferences, honest reasoning has no force. The answer must ground real obligation for persons.

5 Stability
If the base of reality drifts, the rules of logic, meaning, and morals drift too. The answer must be steady in the relevant way.

6 Public intelligibility
Truth should be open to anyone who thinks carefully, not hidden in secret codes. The answer must be public in principle.

7 Embodiment
We use spoken words, written text, and brain activity. Meanings must live in these without being reduced to mere scribbles or firings. The answer must fit a world where signs can carry real meaning.

8 Preservation over time
If meanings and truths can't endure in memory, language, and records, knowledge can't grow. The answer must allow durable transmission.

9 Unified, coherent structure
If there are multiple independent "ultimates," their

clashes would splinter meaning and truth. The answer must be one, coherent, and self-consistent at the root.

10 No shortcuts (no circularity, "just because," private-only, popularity, or vague abstractions)

• No circularity: you can't explain X by quietly assuming X.

• No "just because" (brute fact): that ends the search fo reasons.

• No private-only appeals: what only one person can check cannot bind everyone.

• No popularity votes: many people can agree and still be wrong.

• No foggy labels: saying a fancy word is not an explanation.

Note on Public Revelation

The official seven criteria for the infallible ground of reason include: "Publicly revealed in history and verified by God through repeated, unmistakable miracles (not a private vision or hidden claim)." This is a real and necessary criterion. However, atheists may omit this requirement if they wish. Doing so does not change the outcome: no alternative system satisfies all remaining criteria.

Guidelines for Clear Answers

G1. Name your completely viable candidate in one clear sentence.

G2. For each requirement above, show exactly how your candidate meets it (1–2 sentences per item).

G3. Keep the original meanings of the key terms (truth, meaning, obligation, rational).

G4. No "just because" foundations.

G5. No "true for me" or "works for us" replies.

G6. No private-vision foundations.

G7. If your answer has many independent "ultimates," show why they cannot clash.

G8. Explain embodiment clearly.

G9. Acknowledge the first unmet requirement to avoid endless detours.

Prompts

Full Prompt (tied to all the above standards)
Using the "Question of Questions" standards listed above, name one candidate that satisfies every requirement. Then, in 1–2 sentences per item, show exactly how it meets each requirement, without redefining terms or relying on circularity, brute facts, private experiences, popularity, or vague labels. If it fails any single requirement, identify the first failure and stop.

Single Comprehensive Prompt
Name one candidate that grounds rational thought, and in 1-2 sentences each show how it accounts for

rational thought, shared meaning, universal non-contradictory truth, binding obligations, stability, public intelligibility, embodiment in words, text, and minds, preservation over time, a unified source, avoidance of shortcuts such as circularity, brute facts, private-only appeals, popularity, or fog, and how it is the eternal source of both logic and love, using original meanings of truth, meaning, obligation, and rational, stopping at the first unmet requirement without evasions, disclaimers, or redefinitions.

Single Comprehensive Prompt (Atheist-Friendly Variant)

Name one candidate that grounds rational thought, and in 1–2 sentences each show how it accounts for rational thought, shared meaning, universal non-contradictory truth, binding obligations, stability, public intelligibility, embodiment in words, text, and minds, preservation over time, a unified source, and avoidance of shortcuts such as circularity, brute facts, private-only appeals, popularity, or fog, using original meanings of truth, meaning, obligation, and rational, stopping at the first unmet requirement without evasions, disclaimers, or redefinitions.

(This version omits the requirement of public revelation with divine miracles. Doing so does not alter the outcome.)

www.ingramcontent.com/pod-product-compliance
Lightning Source LLC
Chambersburg PA
CBHW060422050426
42449CB00009B/2087